SEVEN STEPS IN PRACTICAL OCCULTISM

By Paul Foster Case

Edited by Wade Coleman

February 2026 Edition

Copyright by Wade Coleman

Upon my death, this book enters the Public Domain.

ACKNOWLEDGMENTS

I want to thank Your Own World Books for permission to quote from *The Egyptian Text of the Bronzebook*.

Special thanks to Carol Z for her editing.

FOREWORD

Seven Steps to Practical Occultism is perhaps Paul Foster Case's best and worst lesson series. It is best because Seven Steps teaches important techniques. It is the worst because Case leaves out key details. I added notes at the end of the chapters to fill in some of the blanks.

Wade Coleman

May 2020

To contact the author, write to this email.

DENDARA_ZODIAC@protonmail.com

TABLE OF CONTENTS

CHAPTER 1 – What do You Want?
  Chapter 1 Notes
  CHAPTER 2 – Subconscious Powers
  Chapter 2 Notes
CHAPTER 3 – The Subconscious and Its Operations
  Chapter 3 Notes
CHAPTER 4 – Occult Fundamentals
  Chapter 4 Notes
CHAPTER 5 – Crafting Mental Images
  Chapter 5 Notes
CHAPTER 6 - Fixing the Volatile
  Chapter 6 Notes
CHAPTER 7 – Review
  Chapter 7 Notes
PAUL FOSTER CASE BOOKS
WADE COLEMAN BOOKS
BIBLIOGRAPHY

TABLE OF CONTENTS WITH THEMATIC LABELS

1. **What Do You Want?**
   The Power of Purpose and Desire
   Notes: The Laws of Life
2. **Subconsciousness – Part 1**
   Unlocking Inner Power and Memory
   Notes: Deductive Reasoning
3. **Subconsciousness – Part 2**
   Suggestion, Action, and Daily Mental Control
   Notes: Fear is Failure
4. **Occult Fundamentals**
   The Body as the Instrument of Occult Transformation
   Notes: Diet and Health
5. **Crafting Mental Images**
   Visualization and the Reality of Inner Patterning
   Notes: The Four Worlds of the Kabbalah
6. **Subconsciousness – Part 3**
   Transferring Images and Subtle Practices of Influence
   Notes: The Brain
7. **Review**
   Summary of Subconscious Laws and Practical Integration
   Notes: Technique Checklist and Test

CHAPTER 1 – What do You Want?

The practical instruction in this course has one aim. It shows you how to be healthy, happy, and prosperous. It is designed for those interested in applying occultism to their problems. Written for beginners in occult study, it avoids technicalities and speculation, so that those who read it and put it into practice may begin to live the fundamentals it explains.

The welfare of humanity depends on the well-being of the individual units in the social order. This world is good to live in if one knows how to live. These pages outline the forces, laws, and methods that will make you a better and more functional unit in the social order. Put this instruction into practice, and you are doing a service to humanity. When you are happy and prosperous, your daily living will add to the sum of human effectiveness and fulfillment.

True health is contagious. When you express it, your presence is healing. A free, cheerful spirit showers blessings on all who enter its presence. Be full of joy, and you will make your neighbor happy as well. No one lives unto themselves. Apply this knowledge and use the methods provided to succeed, and you will inevitably add to the prosperity of others.

This course is about YOU. By focusing on expressing the incredible powers of human personality, you will help all your relatives, friends, and associates. You will be given clear, specific instructions. Carry them out precisely, giving full attention to every detail.

These pages contain procedures that have been tested and proven. Study each chapter carefully so you know exactly what it means. Then put it into practice. Allow at least a week to work through each lesson. Make haste slowly.

The first step is straightforward yet of utmost importance. Unfortunately, many people never take it. Their failure to take it accounts for their failure in everything else. You may already have attended to this indispensable preliminary. If you have, you will understand how important it is. At the beginning of this study, it is best to reaffirm your decision.

Before you turn this page, take a pencil and paper and write your answer to the question below:

WHAT DO YOU WANT?

By formally making up your mind, you take the first step in the right direction. What you have written is probably rough and far too long a statement. Make a single, concise sentence. Make it a simple goal within your abilities and means to accomplish. Your sentence should give expression to a sole purpose. Begin your sentence; thus, *I will apply all my powers to achieve the following aim.*

Then set down precisely what you wish to accomplish. Remember, your sentence should express a single purpose.

If your ultimate purpose is a long-term project with several intermediate stages, begin by directing your practice toward the first step while keeping the final goal in mind. Then, as soon as the first step is complete, apply your practice to the next. Do not linger by the wayside.

The importance of this first step cannot be overstated. Until you have taken it, read no further. Until ONE PURPOSE, prefaced by the specific declaration of intention given above, is written on paper, you are wasting time and energy by reading any more of this lesson. So stop and do it now.

What I Want, I Really, Really Want

Why do this? Because, provided only that your desire is within the laws of life and justice1, you can be whatever you want to be, do whatever you want to do, and have whatever you want to have.

Note that the echoing verb indicates the imperiousness of craving or need—no puny, timid wishing. A real want has in it the quality of royalty. That is imperious, befitting an emperor or sovereign, commanding. Furthermore, the old Latin root imperative and imperious are verbs meaning "to set in order, to regulate."

This is the magic of a genuine want. It points you in the right direction. It regulates the exercise of all your powers. It brings your life into harmony with the universal order. It prepares you for success because success means "getting things and events to follow one another in the correct sequence."

You can be, do, and have whatever you want because the mental state expressed by this verb always enables you to turn your desire into specific imagery. Wishes are vague. Hopes are hazy. Genuine wants are sharply defined.

Sharp Mental Images Materialize

A clear mental image tends to materialize into an actual condition or event.

Memorize this statement. Explicit images have driving power. Like seeds, they have a life of their own. Use this magic power, and you will take the first step toward bringing them under your direction so you can build with them.

You know what you want! You have chosen your goal. From now on, you will make steady progress toward it. Every stage of the journey is mapped out for you by those who have traveled the road before you. In this instruction, there is no guesswork. It is neither theoretical nor experimental. Thousands who have witnessed their practical value and uplifting power have tried and proven these methods. You are now associated with a company of men and women on the high road to attainment. Their ability is linked to yours through shared interests and the practice of similar methods. You are now engaged with them in a concerted effort to improve humanity by improving its individual units.

No matter how far off your aim may seem, you have turned and faced the right direction today. Unfortunately, most people never take that first step. They have no dominant purpose, planned procedure, or destination. Thus, they never get anywhere. The first step to success is choosing a goal. Otherwise, you go nowhere.

The Power of Action

Mere aspiration will not take you to your chosen goal. So now you must set to work. Eliphas Levi (Alphonse Louis Constant) said,

Every intention that does not assert itself through deeds is vain, and the speech that expresses it is idle. It is an action that proves life and establishes will. Our thoughts and ideas do not judge us, but our works do. We must act to be...

To do a thing, we must believe in the possibility of our doing, and this faith must immediately be translated into action. When a child says, "I cannot," his mother answers, "Try." Faith does not even try; it begins with the certitude of completion and proceeds calmly, as if omnipotence were at its disposal and eternity before it. Dare to formulate your desire, then set to work at once, and do not cease acting in the same manner and for the same end. What you want shall come to pass. It has indeed already begun.

The Great Magical Agent

As if omnipotence were at its disposal. In this phrase, Eliphas Levi tells us a great secret. For omnipotence, or ALL POWER, or the GREAT MAGICAL AGENT, is at our service.

Eliphas Levi describes the ALL POWER as,

There is a force in nature far more powerful than steam. A single person who can master and direct it might throw the world into confusion and transform its face. It is diffused throughout infinity, the substance of heaven and earth. When it produces radiance, it is called light. It is substance and motion at the same time; it is a fluid and a perpetual vibration. The will of intelligent beings acts directly upon this light. By this light, intelligent beings act directly upon nature, which is made subject to the modifications of intelligence.

To master and direct the Great Magical Agent is to accomplish the Great Work, to be master of the world, and to be the depositary even of the power of God.

Being the instrument of life, this force naturally collects at living centers. It cleaves to the kernel of plants as to the heart of man (and the sympathetic nervous system). It identifies with the individual life of the existence it animates. We are saturated with this light and continually project it to make room for more. The settlement and polarization of this light about a center produce a living being. It attracts all the matter necessary to perfect and preserve it.

The Great Magical Agent has four properties: dissolution, consolidation, quickening, and moderation. These four properties, directed by human will, can modify all phases of Nature.

Electricity, which is light when it produces radiance, is considered both a substance (particle) and a motion (wave) simultaneously. Omnipotence is diffused throughout the universe, spanning spaces measured in millions of light-years. From it, the structure of everything in the physical world is built. Using the All Power, we may regulate a room's temperature to produce intense cold in midsummer or torrid heat in midwinter.

Dr. George Crile has offered evidence that the human body is an electrical machine. Moreover, an apparatus has been invented that demonstrates that our bodies are centers of this force, sending off fine radiations imperceptible to ordinary senses.

Manipulating the Great Magical Agent

Human thought and will act directly on the Great Magical Agent. This is why anyone who applies themselves steadily can attain mastery over themselves and their circumstances.

We live in a world of our own creation, built according to our imagined mental pattern.

Change the pattern, and you change the world. You always act directly on this force, which centers itself in you. You do not have to learn how to do this anymore than you must learn how to digest food or teach your heart to beat. Try to get this fact firmly fixed. Every day, up to this moment, you have exercised control over this force and directed it mentally. The world you inhabit now is the one you have built for yourself. If it does not suit you, you can change it.

These lessons do not teach you how to gain power or master hidden forces. You don't need what you already possess. You do not need to become what you are right now. The hidden force always responds to your mental direction. Whatever pattern you impress upon it, that pattern it follows.

The main lesson is to use your power and apply your natural mastery of the Great Magical Agent to produce the desired manifestations. Hence, the primary purpose of these instructions is to teach you how to form the right mental patterns.

Those engaged in this work call themselves Builders of the Adytum. The adytum is the house of God, the inner shrine where divinity dwells. It is also our body, capable of transformation. The housebuilder gathers materials from various places and assembles them according to a plan. So do we take the raw material of human experience and shape it in a particular way. The end sought is to make men and women who are masters of themselves and their surroundings. To attain this end is to know that one is a depositary of the power of God.

To build the adytum, we must learn to control our bodies, direct the nerve currents coursing through them, balance our emotions, and master the mind's modifications.

When you join our enterprise, you have a clear, well-formulated goal, so that even before finishing your study of this first lesson, you have taken a positive step toward your chosen objective.

All the power you need to complete this work is yours NOW—this very minute. After that, you have nothing to acquire but knowledge, and even that is already present in the subconscious treasure house, as described in the next chapter.

Silence is Golden

Crucial instructions have been given in this lesson. Remember to keep your decision to yourself. Do not show anyone what you have written. Do not discuss it at all. Instead, every night before going to bed, read the statement. Do the same every morning before you begin dressing. Then, once you know the words by heart, destroy the paper and recite the speech every night and morning until you have achieved your first objective. Then write a similar statement for the second logical step toward your aim. Once you have realized this, proceed to the third step. Keep your statements of purpose restricted to one at a time.

Always observe this little ritual. It's simple, but it's genuine magic. Always make the definitive introductory statement – I apply all my powers to achieve the following aim. This may seem like a small thing, but as you progress, you'll understand why it's necessary.

Common Mistakes

Over the years, some students have trouble deciding what they want. As a rule, the difficulty stems from setting the aim too far in the future. Some students think they must aim at the highest ideal they can conjure up. This is a grave error. You're to aim at being and doing something to effect a real change in your circumstances.

You may have a glimpse of a relatively distant goal, but the purpose of this technique is to help you progress toward the next definite objective, which appears to lead toward that goal if you see it.

Don't waste a moment trying to think up some lofty, high-flying objective far ahead in life. Life is not lived by years.

It is a matter of days, hours, and minutes. We are not asking you to dedicate yourself to an ideal. Many write us that their one aim is "service," "spiritual enlightenment," or "to know the Truth." None of these is an aim. They are nebulous aspirations, if not symptoms of a desire to "get away from it all."

Example

Let us cite an example. In the summer of 1933, a young woman took this course. Her home life was miserable, with a sick body and a drunken husband. She had no specialized training or money.

When she came to the question, "What do you want?" she said, "I want to be a nurse, but what's the use? No hospital will accept me for training because I never finished high school."

Then she finally decided, "Well, anyway, that's the only thing I want, and that's what I shall try for. Nothing else but!"

It has been some years since that young woman made up her mind. For five years, she has been free of her physical ailments, working as an office nurse and assistant to a physician. Her boss has given her better training for her work with him than she could have secured in any hospital.

Incidentally, she has overcome her educational handicap. During her progress toward her goal, between 1933 and 1939, she opened opportunities for three other women, all of whom could devote full-time to a specialized branch of nursing, which this woman utilized as her first step toward realizing her one aim.

Her environment is altogether better. She has a wide circle of friends. She is entirely different from the sick, miserable, hopeless creature she seemed to be in 1933, a new woman living in a new world shaped by her mental imagery.

Homework

Read this lesson several times during the week to ensure you grasp its full meaning. Pay special attention to the long quotation from Eliphas Levi. It will repay careful study.

Then set down precisely what you wish to accomplish. Remember, your sentence should give expression to a single purpose. Then, begin your statement of purpose; *I will apply all my powers to achieve the following aim.*

Remember that others are working with you. We are all eager to see you reach your chosen goal. You have linked yourself to a great and continually extending chain of intelligent centers of the ALL POWER. We are working with you, and our knowledge and experience will be subtly communicated to you through the contact you have established.

You know what you want. You will achieve it. You dare to aspire to it and work for it. Be sure to remain silent until you have attained your goal.

These lessons teach you a technique to use repeatedly for the rest of your life. It can be applied to every problem and situation you will encounter. It is essential to our work. That's why it comes first.

The techniques you are being taught are Here-and-Now activities. To do them correctly, you must decide on something for which and toward which you can begin to ACT – not later, but NOW.

Chapter 1 Notes

The Laws of Life and Justice

Case says you can be whatever you want to be, do whatever you want to do, and have whatever you want to have. That's a bold statement, but he adds the caveat that your desire must be in line with the laws of life and justice.

In journalism, this is called "bury the lead." Think about it. Before you play a game, you need to know the rules. Why pick an Aim if it's against the rules? Then it is sure to fail. What are these laws of life and justice?

Karma – Enidvadew

Karma means work and action. It's the law of cause and effect. Events are set in motion and may unfold over centuries. Unfortunately, we don't see the big picture of what our soul has set in motion in this life.

In the *Egyptian Texts of the Bronzebook*, I found my best definition of destiny and fate. They also describe a quality called "Enidvadew," which they define as *desires modified by laws*.

The following quotes are from *In the Beginning, Chapter 5.*

Humans, too, are molded by their desires, but unlike the beasts and birds, their yearnings are circumscribed by the laws of fate and destiny and the law of sowing and reaping. These desires, modified by the laws, are called Enidvadew. Unlike the beasts and birds, this in man relates to him rather than to his offspring, though they are not untouched by it.

Destiny may be likened to a man who must travel to a distant city, whether he wishes to make the journey; the destination is his destiny. He may choose whether to go by way of a river or a plain, whether across mountains or through forests, on foot or horseback, slow or fast. Whatever occurs as a result of this decision is fate. If a tree falls on him because he chose the forest path, it is fated, for luck is an element of fate. Destiny leaves no choice; fate offers a limited choice, which may be good or bad, but it cannot be averted. What is fated must be, for there can never be any turning back.

The circumstances of the traveler, Enidvadew, conform to the law of sowing and reaping; he may travel in comfort or pain, happily or sorrowfully, with strength or weakness, heavily burdened or lightly burdened, well prepared or ill-prepared. When the destination is set by the degrees of a former life, the journey's circumstances should conform to the desire. For what use is it to desire a great destination when the law of sowing and reaping decrees that an intolerable burden must be carried on the way? Far better to have lesser aspirations. The decrees of fate are many; the decrees of destiny are few.

In the *Book of Eloma,*

There is also the Great Law to which man must conform; there are intricacies of Enidvadew to be unwoven, and the challenging paths of destiny and fate to be followed. Too often, the price paid for things done or not done is pain and suffering, sorrow, and distress, but where would the benefit be to the debtor if I were to wipe out such debts?

Law, Fate, and Destiny shape your desires. So Case's bold statement that you can be done and have whatever you want is true. But like all truths, it's a half-truth. Another truth is that you can be what your soul wants you to be, do what your soul wants you to do, and be what your soul wants you to be.

And so it goes.

CHAPTER 2 – Subconscious Powers

Your life on earth began with the union of two cells. One carried the essential history of your father's ancestry. The other summarized the life story of your mother's family tree.

When these two cells unite, the subconscious takes command of your body's development. As a result, the subconscious has controlled every function of your organism from that day to this.

We call this mode of life-activity subconsciousness because whatever it does occurs below our level of conscious awareness. Through careful study, psychologists have accumulated knowledge about its powers. This chapter provides the information necessary to proceed toward the attainment of your chosen objective.

After centuries of research on the human body, the sciences of biology, physiology, and organic chemistry remain in their infancy. As a result, we know little about the chemical, mechanical, and physiological transformations that occur in our bodies. It will take centuries before we fully understand all the marvelous processes.

Subconsciousness knows all about these processes. It makes finer adjustments than any machine man has devised. No chemist can duplicate some of the wonders our glands perform daily. Subconsciousness does this for an infant savage or an adult scientist. None of these marvels of body control depends on our conscious knowledge.

The subconscious cures every disease. Medicines do not heal. They initiate a chemical reaction to which the real healing power responds; whatever that is, it is hidden in the subconscious. Surgery does not heal. Neither makes mechanical adjustments. They remove obstacles to the free manifestation of the hidden curative power.

This power can be awakened through mental methods, which often succeed where drugs, surgery, and adjustments have failed. Please do not misunderstand us. We are not a healing cult. However, mental methods have cured diseases when ether therapy has failed. Shall we abandon other systems of treatment? By no means. You will learn practical, sane ways to use the curative mental force to help yourself and others.

The subconscious healing power is not limited to curing functional and nervous ills. Stubborn organic ailments are sometimes cured by mental means, but why not always? The honest answer is that we don't know. In this course, we will tell you what we do know.

Subconsciousness and Memory

Subconsciousness keeps a perfect record of all our experiences. Whatever affects our senses leaves a subconscious impression, and when the right conditions are provided, any detail of our past may be recalled. The secret of a good memory is not about retaining impressions but about making clear ones, relating them properly together, and bringing them to the surface of consciousness when needed.

When you know the secret of recollection, you have at your disposal the wealth of experience stored in your mind from acts of conscious attention. Practice will enable us to use the greater treasure of the immense number of impressions recorded without our conscious knowledge.

Furthermore, the subconscious organizes and processes the mass of mental records and appears to have the power to think. This subconscious reasoning has certain limitations. It is restricted to deduction1, that is, drawing conclusions from premises. Unconscious thought processes elaborate on every conclusion drawn from a given premise. This deductive process yields both false and true assumptions. This is why there are so many sham doctrines and superstitions. However logical a series of deductions may be, they are worth nothing unless the initial premise is correct. You must guard against the subconscious's tendency to accept false assumptions. Thus, you can use your subconscious thinking processes safely and constructively.

Instincts and Intuitions come through Subconsciousness.

Instincts, so to speak, come from below and are part of our subconscious inheritance from the past. Intuitions come through the subconscious, but from the super-consciousness.

When Zerah Colburn, at the age of eight, could give the square root of 106,929 instantly, without stopping to think, the superconscious perception of mathematical truth was transmitted to his conscious mind through the channel of the subconscious.

Children could play intricate pieces almost as soon as they could sit at a piano. Others excelled at musical composition before reaching their teens. Leaders in every field have testified that "something tells" them the most valuable things they know in their unique lines of endeavor. For example, the Sumerian cuneiform language was deciphered because Rawlinson guessed that the phrase "king of kings" would frequently occur in the inscriptions. The phrase was isolated, and its decipherment led to the recovery of the whole writing system. Such guesses come to us from something outside our normal mental processes. For practical purposes, that something is subconscious and can be controlled.

Those who develop an unusual skill learn that this is true. The best billiard shots, the most spectacular plays in sports, and the brilliant flashes of genius displayed by a master of chess are manifestations of the subconscious. So many of the best things said come straight from the subconscious. Here, too, a writer finds his best inspirations.

This is not all. With the determination to realize it, selecting a definite aim sets hidden forces in motion, providing us with the necessary materials and connecting us with the people we need to meet to attain our goal.

Not long before his death, Edison gave an interview in which he spoke of the success of his friend, Henry Ford. "Henry? Why Henry taps the subconscious." Mr. Ford said that whenever we decide to do something and stick to our decision, we send out mental entities that connect us with others and bring us the resources we need to execute our plans.

No completely satisfactory explanation of this hidden operation of our subconsciousness has been advanced. Many attempts have been made to account for the facts. Books on New Thought and Mentalism have put forward a theory called the "Law of Attraction." There are other plausible and reasonable theories, and others are highly fantastic. What we know boils down to this:
Something within us, below the surface, connects us to whatever we need to be, want to be, do, and have. This

something can be put into action by anyone who learns and practices the techniques.

These subconscious operations are manifestations of the Great Magical Agent. Certain books suggest that the art of directing and using this inner force is not new. In every age, some people understood this art and left records whose essence is contained in this instruction.

Some of these records have unusual forms, but we have keys to their meaning. Therefore, we can give you clear instructions on how to train your mind and body to realize your life's aim.

This technique is a practical art of life, subjected to rigorous tests. Modern science explains some of it, but not all. Fortunately, complete explanations of the effectiveness of specific practices are not required to teach the methods.

Powers of Subconsciousness

A child may learn to swim even without scientific knowledge of the laws of physics. Likewise, you can learn to manage your latent powers, even if you do not always understand why your practice produces the results it does.

Focus your attention on the powers you can use immediately to achieve your chosen objective. When you direct your subconscious, you employ forces that can enable you:

1. To keep your body functioning efficiently.

2. To develop your intuitive understanding of the laws of nature that you employ to achieve your ONE AIM;

3. To get in touch with the people and resources you need to reach your chosen goal.

Your statement in Chapter One means more than you may initially realize. When you say, "I will apply ALL my powers," you include mighty subconscious forces and other powers of the personality. In choosing your specific object, you have set in motion the subconscious agency that has helped thousands of people grow in wisdom, power, and happiness.

You can use the Great Magical Agent and direct its currents toward every conceivable right end. It is yours to command and employ to produce revolutionary changes in your personality and circumstances. You are now part of an organized movement that uses these subconscious potencies daily, every hour of the day.

Some of the achievements of persons connected with this movement have been astounding. Yet they have been accomplished by people no more gifted than you.

Devote a full week to studying this lesson. Continue making your declaration of purpose every morning and every night. As you say the words, remember that they are planting potent suggestions in your subconscious, which will be fully responsive.

Chapter 2 Notes

Deductive Reasoning

The subconscious possesses powers of deductive reasoning.

In *deductive reasoning*, conclusions are drawn from a data set. For example:

All men (A) are mortal (B).   1st premise
Socrates (C) is a man (A).   2nd premise
Therefore, Socrates (C) is mortal (B).   Conclusion

Or,

If A = B   1st premise
If C = A   2nd premise
Therefore, C = B   Conclusion

Inductive reasoning draws broad generalizations from specific observations. For example, you have a bag of coins. The first three coins you pull out are pennies. Therefore, you conclude that all coins in the bag are pennies. Of course, the premise that all coins in the bag are pennies may or may not be accurate.

CHAPTER 3 – The Subconscious and Its Operations

In Chapter Two, you learned about the subconscious and its powers. The law that enables you to make the best and fullest use of your subconscious power may be stated as:

SUBCONSCIOUSNESS IS ALWAYS AMENABLE TO CONTROL BY SUGGESTION.

This lesson will help you take advantage of its operation. But first, let's make sure you understand the previous statement.

The Standard Dictionary defines *amenable* as,

1. Subject to authority; easily persuaded or controlled.

2. Submissive; tractable.

All these shades of meaning apply to amenable in connection with the subconscious.

You can call the subconscious to account whenever it seems to fall short in its work. It is always subject to your authority. It is submissive and tractable. Its response to your authority is neither grudging surrender nor unwillingness. It is easily led and directed. The ease with which you can manage its operations is astounding.

Much of what is written about the subconscious gives the impression that controlling its activities is difficult. Nothing could be further from the truth. On the contrary, the subconscious is easy to manage and never resists our efforts to control it.

Because it's easy to govern, the subconscious often seems extremely stubborn. Whenever we think of the subconscious as resistant, it takes the suggestion and resists it until we give it a definite counter-suggestion. The subconscious is easy to manage once you know how.

Control of any force means exerting a directing or restraining influence over it. This needs emphasis. Subconsciousness cannot direct itself. Much less can it lead us. Therefore, its extraordinary powers must always be limited if they are to do us any good.

The free expression of the subconscious is insanity. Unfortunately, state hospitals house many people who surrender to the unrestrained impulses of the subconscious. No one can gain health, success, or happiness by letting the subconscious run wild.

On the other hand, control does not mean meddlesome interference. We must give directions, but we must be careful to leave this inner, deeper mind free to obey our instructions in its own way. Suppose we want health. We know that the subconscious carries out all the body-building work. Our concern is not with the processes but with their outcome.

Therefore, the second point is this:

Your conscious work ends when you formulate a clear, distinct image of your desire and hand it over to the subconscious to be acted upon.

Fear is Failure[1]

Take care to express perfect confidence in the powers of the subconscious. For example, doubt or anxiety about results, or indulging in too many repetitions of suggestions, impresses a fear pattern. Then the subconscious immediately goes to work to materialize the fear pattern it has received.

That's why you need to understand Chapter 2 before moving forward. The knowledge of the powers of the subconscious in Chapter 2 will help you banish moods of doubt or anxiety. When you know what the subconscious can do, you will be confident that your demands will be fulfilled.

What is a *Suggestion*?

Regarding the meaning of suggestion, there is confusion of tongues. Some say that a suggestion is anything that makes an impression on the subconscious. This is true, but it's vague. What we need to know is what makes the necessary impression.

Others say a suggestion is a command impressed on the mind during mesmeric or hypnotic states. Such states are the result of suggestion, and except in the abnormal conditions they present, subconsciousness is NOT amenable to direct commands.

A good suggestion requires subtlety. A suggestion is a hint. In a negative sense, it is an insinuation. An effective suggestion is indirect. The subconscious responds more readily to what is implied than to what is explicitly affirmed, stated, or commanded.

It does this because subconscious reasoning is deductive. It is natural for this part of your mind to work out hints and draw them to their logical conclusions. You must consider this characteristic to use your subconscious powers to the best advantage.

A SUGGESTION IS ANYTHING THAT HINTS AT THE SUBCONSCIOUS, THE DESIRED RESPONSE.

You do not have to coerce the subconscious. However, an effective suggestion must state what you want done in a gentle way. Hence, the Emerald Table says, suavely and with great ingenuity.

Now you understand that the subconscious is always amenable to control by suggestion. All the powers described in Chapter 2 are yours to direct. The responsibility for directing them properly lies with you. When you work with it correctly, your subconscious is always responsive and easy to govern. What you have now to learn and practice is the art of conveying to the subconscious the kind of impressions that indicate what must be done.

Gaining proficiency in this art takes time and perseverance, but the work is not difficult. What makes subconsciousness seem difficult is ignorance of the correct procedure.

Quacks exploit this ignorance. They claim only their methods work. They spread the false notion that controlling the subconscious is arduous, challenging, and perhaps dangerous.

It is nothing of the kind. You have been controlling your subconscious by suggestion all your life. You have been giving your willing servant positive and negative hints.

The result of its perfect obedience depends on the suggestions given.

For instance, we all want perfect health; you may have tried many methods. Many people use affirmations or statements intended to influence their subconscious. If you have succeeded, it is because you gave useful suggestions. If you failed, your affirmations and commands were counteracted by the suggestive power of your habitual ways of thinking, imagining, speaking, and acting.

Even a perfectly conceived suggestion for health will fail if it is contradicted by hundreds of fear thoughts, by persistent carelessness in food selection, or by a refusal to give your body its necessary supplies of water, air, and light.

WHAT YOU DO AND THINK ALL DAY LONG IS RECORDED IN SUBCONSCIOUSNESS.

The most potent message you can send to your subconscious is your actions. If your deeds do not match your words, the suggestion that reaches and affects our inner consciousness is the suggestion of our ACTIONS, not that of the statements or affirmations.

Making a mental pattern of perfect health and denying your body the materials to build it gives your subconscious the strongest counter-suggestion. Instead of health, you really want a disease. Then you get what you ask for.

Formulating a mental pattern for success in a business venture is essential. However, the subconscious will not work on that pattern if you foolishly spend the resources you possess. Nor will the subconscious build your business if you allow your home and office to be in disorder. Success and order are synonyms. Until you keep order as well as you can, with what you have now, all the success suggestions will be outweighed by the subtle hints of failure conveyed by the disorderly condition of your surroundings.

These examples are intended to make it clear that the subconscious is not only amenable to suggestions at certain times but is always amenable and obeys the predominant suggestion. There is no magic formula for success if you are disorderly. For example, if you want to stay healthy, do not neglect hygiene. You will not be happy if you persist in negatively interpreting your experience.

Subconsciousness is Controlled from the Level of Self-conscious Awareness

What we think, say, and do throughout the day make up the bulk of the impressions received by the subconscious. First, therefore, we must consider our bodies. Then we need to pay attention to our speech. After this, we shall be ready to watch our thoughts.

The work begins with our bodies because all we accomplish must be done through their instrumentality. This is not a course on diet or hygiene, and it will not go into detail on those matters. What is necessary to say here is to get the facts about your body's needs for food, water, air, and light – the facts, not the fantastic theories of faddists and quacks. Then put that knowledge into practical use.

By doing so, you give your subconscious the strongest possible hint that you want it to build a healthy body. Later, you will receive instructions on forming the right mental patterns. But remember that you cannot build a healthy body without the necessary materials, just as you cannot build a house merely by looking at the architect's plans.

Once you have learned the requirements for building a healthy body, focus on your environment. Begin with your clothes. Make sure they are clean and well cared for. Next, ensure your home is clean and orderly, especially where you sleep. Your workspace should also be clean and orderly, even if you are not free to express your ideas. The details you are responsible for can be kept in order. Follow these simple rules, and you will give your subconscious the most potent and successful suggestions.

What to do to control words and thoughts will be explained in later chapters. However, skill in constructive speech and the formulation of creative ideas comes from practices that require extended description.

Begin at once to put the counsel of this lesson into practice. Thus, you will take your first steps toward success.

Chapter 3 Notes

Fear is Failure[1]

When practicing the visualization technique, don't start with something that carries a strong emotional charge. Begin with something simple. It could be as simple as finding a penny, getting a phone call, or spotting the woodpecker that makes all the racket in the morning.

Keep this exercise fun and straightforward.

Suggesting is a Hint[2]

Case says a good suggestion needs a degree of subtlety. Therefore, a suggestion is a hint about what you want.

For example, I pulled my bicep muscle. One suggestion is that I apply all my power to achieve the following aim: my bicep muscles are whole and well; however, this is not a hint.

A better suggestion would be to fill my bicep muscles with healing light. Then, through deductive reasoning, my subconscious acts upon my suggestion.

Include Other People

When you visualize your one Aim, include other people. How do others benefit when you achieve your goal? For example, if you want a car, is it just for you, or for your family? Even if the car is just for you, your employer benefits because you have reliable transportation to get to work.

Including other people in your One Aim serves two purposes. First, considering other people in your Aim increases the number of connections the subconscious can make. Second, the technique helps us see personal greed. This technique doesn't work all the time, but it's useful when you're dreaming of big-ticket items.

The Magical Vision

Then comes the work of cultivating the magical vision. First, consider the premise that magic always works, but never the way you expect it to. Do you have the eyes to see and the heart to recognize when your One Aim has manifested?

If you aimed for a car and got a scooter, that's a success. Don't beat yourself up when you don't get exactly what you want. If you have a dog and ask him to fetch your slippers, and he brings back a ball, do you scold the dog? Of course not. It's cute. When your subconscious doesn't bring you exactly what you visualized, thank it very nicely and try again. Don't beat up your subconscious when it "fails."

CHAPTER 4 – Occult Fundamentals

WHATEVER YOU DO TO ACHIEVE THE AIM YOU HAVE FORMULATED MUST BE DONE THROUGH SOME FORM OF BODILY ACTIVITY.[1]

Is this truth so self-evident as to be hardly worth mentioning? Yet experience shows that few people consider it or fully understand all it implies. Nothing is more common than neglecting this first principle of the art of living. Hence, during practical instruction, the need to stress the importance of this principle.

Thinking is as much a bodily action as chopping down a tree. The most important kind of physical activity is thought. To make our thinking more productive, understand that thinking is a function of the brain, as breathing is a function of the lungs.

Every function of the human personality is performed by a group of cells. Your body contains about thirty trillion cells. Their operation is the basis of what you think, say, and do. The fulfillment of your one aim is achieved through cellular action. The power expressed through thirty trillion cells enables you to be what you want to be, do what you want to do, and have what you want to have. What is this power?

Organic and Inorganic Life

Both scientists and occultists agree that life arises when certain chemical elements are arranged in specific patterns. Some structures are adapted to manifesting life. We call these structures that manifest life 'organic,' such as animals or plants. Other structures cannot manifest life and are therefore latent. These are inorganic matter. However, they are composed of the same chemical elements as organic life. Their differences are structural. This is a very ancient occult doctrine.

Light-power or Life-power

Every cell is composed of chemical elements. These elements, and the water in which they are dissolved, are composed of smaller structures called atoms.

The real substance of every atom is radiant energy or light, sometimes called electromagnetism. These are different names, for one thing. Thus, the material of the cells of your body is light-power. Furthermore, the energy that manifests as activity in these cells is the same as light-power. The function of every cell results from the light-power flowing through it.

This light-power is also the substance of everything else in the universe. All existence is a mode of it. It is the power behind chemical reactions in inorganic materials. The same power expresses itself through plants, the human body, and, primarily, the human brain, producing human personality.

Radiant energy builds the structure of inorganic forms and our bodies. Radiant energy sustains the functions of plants, animals, and humans. This light-power must also be the Life-power, since living beings' mental and physical activities are included in its manifestation.

Life-power is both the substance and the active force in every cell of our bodies. Yet this power is not limited to those cells or to the various structures in our environment. Hence, Eliphas Levi wrote, "It is distributed throughout infinity; it is the substance of heaven and earth."

Life-power builds all physical structures, including the cells of our bodies, from itself. The physical universe is not the outcome of Life-power's action upon a second-something-called matter. The one something in the universe is the single conscious energy of Life-power.

Consider consciousness to be one pole of this single reality. In this course, *Consciousness* also means *Spirit*. *Energy* means *Working Power*. All forms and objects express this working power and the reality behind physical matter. By acting upon itself, the Life-power brings all types of force into being and produces all varieties of structure.

When the Life-power works through your muscles, they contract, causing many complex chemical and electrical changes. When the same power operates through your brain cells and other centers of your nervous system, it manifests as certain states of consciousness and the expression of human personality capabilities associated with those mental states.

It's taken millions of years to bring the human organism to its present state of development. However, development has not ceased. Dr. Frederick Tilney says that in ages to come, we shall develop brain centers that will enable us to exercise powers we cannot even dream of now.

The Great Work

Every generation produces men and women who can exercise unusual mental and physical powers. They live today, and one purpose of this course is to add to their number. Their exceptional command over themselves, their influence on others, and their great control of nature's forces result from a higher order of brain development than that of most people.

Furthermore, these unusual men and women have developed practices. This personal training system transforms the body so that anyone who does the work can exercise powers comparable to those of the Inner School members.

The physical transformations are chemical and structural. Some of these practices aim to change the composition of the blood, lymph, and glandular secretions. Other phases of the work are designed to alter the composition of cell groups in the brain and the nervous system.

To apply these practices, we must recognize that we are not working on some vague, invisible entity called the *mind*. Instead, we shall produce a series of changes in our bodies to specialize the Life-power into modes of force that are not expressed through the average human organism.

To effect these changes, refer to chapter three, since the subconscious is the bodybuilder and is always amenable to suggestion. When we know how to give it the right kind of hints, we can set it to work on processes that will bring about the chemical and structural modifications mentioned.

We can do this because we possess knowledge of the undertaking. However, because of this work's nature, this knowledge remained in the hands of a few people until recently. Even now, relatively few students are ready to receive technical instruction.

In former times, the human race's general ignorance made it dangerous for those possessing this knowledge to communicate it. Not because they wished to keep it to themselves, but because their efforts to teach it met with ridicule, persecution, and organized resistance. The wise were forced to conceal their true opinions from the masses.

Ignorance and intolerance are still at work globally, but their power is less than it once was. Over the past fifty years [written CIRCA 1936], there has been an advance in knowledge and general education that now makes it possible to speak more openly than before. To some extent, what was formerly written in parables, paradoxes, and enigmas may now be stated without disguise. Much that was formerly limited to symbolic expression, understood by initiates only, is now reported in plain language.

Such direct, open expression of esoteric doctrine is the aim of the texts in our curriculum. In this chapter, you have the fundamental idea at the heart of occult teachings.

Through patience and practice, the wise agreed that humanity could use the Great Magical Agent or Life-power to free ourselves from the shackles of poverty, disease, and failure. It is the one Conscious Energy that manifests as light and life throughout the universe.

This was the ancient teaching of India, Persia, Egypt, and the Greeks. It is the doctrine of the Bible. Hermes Trismegistus sums it up: "All things are from One, by the mediation of One, and all things have their birth from this One Thing by adaptation."

Through the ages, wise men agree that liberation is achieved by altering the physical body's chemistry and structure to make it a more effective vehicle for expressing the limitless possibilities of Life-power.

Central to all this teaching is that these methods for changing the body's chemistry and structure are mostly, but not wholly, mental. Before any mental work may be undertaken, it is necessary to bring the body to a degree of health.

The First Rule is Cleanliness, Inner as well as Outer

Those who master themselves and their circumstances must drink enough water to provide their glands with the fluid needed to secrete the complex substances they pour into the blood. You must know enough about diet so you are fed rather than poisoned. You must learn to breathe deeply and practice until breathing is regular and rhythmic. You must teach them the proper posture so they habitually stand erect. No details are given here because you can find what you need to know with a little research. If you don't make the effort required to gain this preliminary information and put it into practice, you will not be ready for more advanced instruction.

Attend Your Body

Mental practice will be discussed in the next three chapters. However, mental training is of little use to one who will not use their brain to attend to the preliminaries described. *Furthermore, mental exercises are valid only when the body is supplied with the right food, sufficient water, and enough pure air.*[2] Sometimes, mental practice is dangerous until the body is cleansed of accumulated toxins.

It is assumed you'll treat your body respectfully and give it what it needs. From now on, your instruction is the mental work required to bring your subconscious under your direction. From the precious treasure of occult lore handed down by the wise, you will receive clear and explicit instructions to set your feet on the path leading to your goal.

Homework

As preparation, spend a week considering which body activities are required to realize your heart's desire. If you have difficulty, it's probably because your aim is not sufficiently concrete or you are trying to see too far ahead.

Remember, you want to be and do, and being and doing are always expressed through bodily action. So what will your body have to do next? What physical actions must you perform? Is your body ready for those actions? If not, what must be changed to make it ready?

Consider carefully so you know what your body has to accomplish. Then you can judge whether your physical organism can comfortably carry out its part in realizing your purpose. If you find it deficient in any way, your *next step is to improve it*. This will lay the foundation for all future buildings.

Chapter 4 Notes

Symbolic Acts[1]

Case says, "Whatever you do to realize the Aim you have formulated must be accomplished through some body activity."

Besides thinking and visualizing, there are other activities you can perform. That activity can symbolize what you want, like a car. What would the key feel like between your fingers? Physicality involves rotating your wrist and turning the ignition. That's a symbolic act and a form of bodily activity.

Diet and Health[2]

Case says to do your own research on diet. However, there is a lot of noise-to-signal on the internet, making it difficult to determine what is essential. Below is my shortlist of diet advice.

Sugar and Fructose

Sugar is an energy source that our bodies can easily convert into energy. Unfortunately, most soft drinks contain high-fructose corn syrup. Only liver cells can break down fructose. The end products are triglycerides (fat), uric acid, and free radicals. These byproducts cause inflammation. Triglycerides in the bloodstream can contribute to plaque buildup in the arterial walls. Free radicals can damage cell structures, enzymes, and DNA. Uric acid can inhibit nitric oxide production, which helps protect arterial walls from damage.

The American Heart Association recommends that our diet contain no more than 5% to 7.5% added sugar.

> "Overall, the odds of dying from heart disease rose in tandem with the percentage of sugar in the diet—and that was true regardless of a person's age, sex, physical activity level, and body-mass index (a measure of weight)." – Harvard Health Publishing

Artificial sweeteners are not much better. Instead, they play a trick on our bodies. Research suggests that artificial sweeteners may prevent our bodies from associating sweetness with caloric intake. Therefore, we crave more sweets, choose sweet foods over nutritious foods, and gain weight. The US National Library of Medicine National Institute of Health has this to say:

"Our findings demonstrate that intense sweetness can surpass cocaine reward, even in drug-sensitized and addicted individuals. We speculate that the addictive potential of intense sweetness stems from an inborn hypersensitivity to sweet tastants. In most mammals, including rats and humans, sweet receptors evolved in ancestral environments low in sugar and are thus not adapted to high concentrations of sweet tastants. The supranormal stimulation of these receptors by sugar-rich diets, such as those now widely available in modern societies, would generate a supranormal reward signal in the brain, with the potential to override self-control mechanisms and lead to addiction".

Protein

Whether vegetarian or omnivore, you need protein to grow and rebuild cells.

The best meat is pasture-raised. Animals give their lives so humans can live. At the very least, we can give these animals the respect they deserve by raising them in the most natural conditions possible.

Veganism

In the United States, 94% of soy is genetically modified to withstand the herbicide glyphosate. Glyphosate is a known risk factor for Non-Hodgkin Lymphoma. Glyphosate is absorbed by soybeans and enters our bodies when we eat them.

Vegetarian

Plants don't like being eaten, so they bind their nutrients, making them hard to digest.

"Natural toxins may be present in plants. They are usually metabolites produced by plants to defend themselves against threats such as bacteria, fungi, insects, and predators, and may be species-specific, contributing to the plant's characteristics, e.g., colors and flavors. Common examples of natural toxins in food plants include lectins in beans such as green beans, red kidney beans, and white kidney beans; cyanogenic glycosides in bitter apricot seeds, bamboo shoots, cassava, and flaxseeds; glycoalkaloids in potatoes; 4'-methoxy pyridoxine in ginkgo seeds; colchicine in fresh lily flowers; and muscarine in some wild mushrooms."
– Natural Toxins in Food Plants, Centre for Food Safety, Government of Hong Kong.

When we are younger, our bodies can more efficiently digest and absorb the nutrients we need. However, as we age, our enzyme levels decline, making it harder to digest food. Therefore, vegetarians and vegans should take protein, Vitamin D, and B supplements.

Supplements

The Mayo Clinic recommends that everyone eat 2 ½ cups of vegetables daily. However, most people, including me, don't come close to that amount. Therefore, I take a multivitamin and minerals.

Vitamin D is not found in many foods, so many people are deficient, especially in the wintertime when you bundle up and don't get much sunlight. Low levels of Vitamin D in the bloodstream are linked to age-related diseases, including cancer, vascular disease, and inflammation. Our Vitamin D levels depend on sunlight. Therefore, studies have shown that infections increase during the winter months.

The official minimum daily requirement for Vitamin D is 600 units. However, this is the minimum—getting a blood test is the best way to assess your Vitamin D levels. Levels below 20 ng/mL are considered deficient. Life Extension Magazine recommends Vitamin D levels above 50 ng/mL. Vitamin D is a fat-soluble molecule, so it's best to take it with the largest meal of the day. The only way to know your Vitamin D level is to get a blood test.

Remember, the most direct suggestion you can send to your subconscious is the right selection of food and drink. Eating healthy foods tells your subconscious you want health and wellness rather than sickness and disease.

Also, you cannot change habit patterns unless you provide your body with proper nutrition. Eliminating old patterns releases toxins into your bloodstream, which must be cleared. To build healthy new patterns, you need to eat healthy foods.

To want a healthy body while living on a junk food diet is to lie to yourself. The subconscious is always amenable to control by suggestion. The foods we eat and our environment are the most potent influences on the subconscious.

One Last Thing

There are many people with strong opinions about everything, including food. Master Jesus said, "A man is not defiled by what enters his mouth, but by what comes out of it." – Matthew 15:11.

CHAPTER 5 – Crafting Mental Images

You never have to lie to your subconscious to set it to work, building the conditions to transform your desire from a mental fact into a physical reality.

Be sure you understand this. You do not attempt to deceive your subconscious. Instead, you learn the truth about yourself, tell yourself that truth, and act on it.

The Truth Sets You Free

All that keeps anyone sick, miserable, or in want is ignorance of human personality, its place in the scheme of things, and its powers. This ignorance colors and shapes the suggestions that continually pass from our self-conscious minds to our subconscious. It makes us tell ourselves lies. Because the subconscious is always amenable to suggestion, these lies become patterns that it proceeds to work out. *The remedy is the truth.*

People accept the lie that sickness is expected, and the subconscious does its best to fulfill that expectation. They accept the lie that all resources and opportunities belong to a few lucky individuals. Because they expect to be poor, the subconscious gives that expectation form. They accept the lie that happiness is for the few, and the subconscious builds on that pattern, bringing misery.

The truth is that sickness should be a rare exception. We have every reason to expect continual good health. The truth is that there is more than enough wealth for everybody—an inexhaustible supply. It is always available to anyone who knows how to access it. The truth is that anyone can be happy when they learn and live by the laws of their nature. An occult aspirant trains themself to expect health and to create specific images of prosperity and happiness.

We do not attempt to deceive the subconscious. Knowledge of our mental activities enables us to understand that we possess power, wisdom, and the resources sufficient to manifest any desirable condition. Through the subconscious, we are in touch with the raw material required to transform the forms or conditions we desire into physical realities in our environment.

In their workshop, a goldsmith knows the raw gold on their bench, the tools, and their skill. Already, the beautiful chalice presents itself to their mind's eye.

It is conceded that many people's outward circumstances seem to contradict the conditions they desire. For example, millions of people are sick, poor, and unhappy. However, we know that the power that enters every human life through the subconscious can fully change these conditions.

Mental Images Are Real

At this moment, you possess all you want as a mental fact. A mental fact is as real as a physical fact. However, you can't wear a mental dress or ride in a mental automobile. Yet you will never wear the garment nor drive the physical car until you grasp and apply the truth that the mental picture of a desirable condition is a *real possession*, which you must cling to until it is materialized as a physical actuality.

Keep your mental pattern steady before your mind's eye. Think of it as a real, present reality. Dream of it. Dwell upon it. Perfect its details. Then turn it over to your subconscious, as explained in this lesson and the following lessons. Then, as sure as day follows night, what you created mentally will be experienced as a visible, tangible physical reality.

Visualization, or the creation of explicit mental images, is most important in practical occultism. The more detailed the picture, the clearer the pattern. Sir Francis Galton wrote:

The free action of a vivid visualizing faculty is important in connection with the higher processes of generalized thought. A visual image is a perfect form of mental representation whenever the shape and spatial relations of objects are concerned. The best workers are those who visualize what they propose to do before taking a tool into their hands. Strategists, artists of all denominations, physicists who contrive new experiments... and all who do not follow a routine need it. A faculty of importance in the technical and artistic occupations, which gives accuracy to our perceptions and justice to our generalizations, is starved by lazy disuse.

By deciding what you want next, you take the first step toward forming mental images that the subconscious will materialize. Later, you will be instructed on how to complete those images and shown how to imbue them with the suggestive magical power that rouses the subconscious to bring them into tangible physical form.

Whatever your aim may be, when accomplished, it will take a physical form. What will it be? Take a pencil and paper and write down your responses to the following questions.

1. WHAT COLORS ARE THE THING WHICH EMBODIES YOUR DESIRES?

Suppose you want a healthy body. Your mental image must include the rosy glow of health in the cheeks, the bright whiteness of the eyeballs, the wholesome tint of normal skin, and the healthy translucence of fingernails. These are a few of the color details of a healthy body. If your aim is health, discover others and incorporate them into your image.

Suppose you want a house. What color should it be on the outside? What color scheme should the rooms have? What color scheme should the furniture have?

Suppose you want to "be of service" or "evolve spiritual consciousness." Those are good aims, but they are too indefinite in this form. To be of service means doing something. What are the physical details? What colors do those details have? Evolving spiritual consciousness will affect your body and its surroundings. Find the shades that match that difference.

2. WHAT ARE THE SOUNDS CHARACTERISTIC OF THE EMBODIMENT OF YOUR DESIRE?

If health is your aim, how does the voice of a healthy person sound? At first, you may not think of sound images connected to a house. But if that is what you are aiming at, *try*. You will be amazed. No matter what you want, sounds relate to it. Imagine them.

3. WHAT MOVEMENTS WILL BE MANIFESTED BY THE MATERIALIZATION OF YOUR DESIRE?

Here is the scope for a great many vivid details.

4. WHAT MATERIALS WILL IT BE COMPOSED OF?

Are they coarse or fine? Hard or soft? Warm or cold? Light or heavy? Plastic or metal?

5. WHAT OTHER SENSATIONS, BESIDES THOSE INCLUDED, WILL THE THING YOU WANT AROUSE?

Go over every detail of your image. Write each one down on paper. Use specific words. If you describe a color, identify it. Consider size and weight; be specific.

Working with pencil and paper will make your mental image clearer and more vivid. *The details of the movement are particularly important.* For example, if you want a house, include movement. See yourself approaching from the street, entering the front door, and walking through every room. See yourself in each room, doing what it's intended for. The more detail you put into the imagery, the better!

MAKE YOUR IMAGE IN THE **PRESENT** TENSE.

See your image as a present reality. If your image concerns a project or a personal relationship, mentally go through the various actions involved. See these mental images for what they are, present realities on the mental plane.[1]

This is a mental operation. Your mental pictures are realities you possess when you contemplate them. They may be outlines or living photographs. If they are living pictures in three dimensions, with solidity, weight, form, color, and action, they will materialize more rapidly than mere outline sketches in black and white. Follow the instructions carefully, and your first attempts will have a lot of body and color. Eventually, you will find yourself creating mental sculptures rather than rough sketches on a flat surface.

This practice of forming mental images yields tangible results. It is not the same as the imagery that calls forth subconscious powers to manifest. That is another kind of imagery described in chapter seven.

For now, practice seeing what you want and keeping it before your mind's eye as a reality. Devote at least a week to following these instructions.

In this chapter, you learned how to form mental patterns. In chapter six, you will be taught how to transfer them to the subconscious.

Chapter 5 Notes

Four Worlds of the Kabbala

The four worlds of the Kabbalah are:

World	Hebrew	Meaning	Plane
Atziluth	אֲצִילוּת	Aristocracy, nobility, *emanation*. *Closeness.*	Pure Spirit
Briah	בְּרִיאָה	*Creation*, making; the world, cosmos.	Higher Mind
Yetzirah	יְצִירָה	*Formation.*	Lower Mind
Assiah	עֲשִׂיָּה	Act, action, doing, making, performance.	Physical

Technically, there are five worlds. The highest is Adam Kadmon, but this world is so transcendent that it's difficult to describe and is often omitted.

Mental images are real on the Yetziratic plane, while our physical bodies dwell in Assiah.

CHAPTER 6 - Fixing the Volatile

Transferring Images to Subconsciousness

The subconscious responds better to suggestion than to direct command. However, it is necessary to transfer a specific image of the desired result into the subconscious.

This image is not a command. Your statement formulates your will and desire but does not attempt to dictate to the subconscious how your desire is transformed into an external reality.

The specific image is necessary because it evokes subconscious associations. Your hidden powers are brought into play through these associations, not by forcing the subconscious into specific kinds of activity.

Remember, the subconscious is always below the level of conscious thought. Just as you cannot see the transformations that turn a seed into a plant, you cannot see the subconscious's hidden workings. It is unprofitable to pry into them. What you need is a practical method for planting your mental seed. This seed is a specific image of what you want.

When you have formulated your mental picture, use pencil and paper to record as many details as you can about weight, size, color, action, etc. Then you may begin transferring this image to the subconscious.

Silence

Let us repeat the caution from Chapter One. *Maintain strict silence about your Aim.* This principle of absolute reserve is among the most important in practical psychology. Conserve the energy others waste discussing what they intend to do.

The Bible is full of psychology, noting that the tongue is an unruly member. Discussing your plans dissipates the energy needed to carry them to a successful conclusion. Remember, the world belongs to the silent ones. Maintaining silence builds power, both physical and psychological. Observe this rule carefully.

Meditation

Set aside a few minutes every day. Go to a room free of interruptions and sit in a comfortable, straight-backed chair. Don't cross your legs. Let your hands rest comfortably in your lap. Sit erect, with your head, neck, and back in a straight line.

Do not relax, neither be tense. The right posture is one in which every voluntary muscle is free from strain yet fully alive.

Repeat your statement of purpose once, firmly and vigorously. Then, unless you are likely to be overheard, say it aloud.

Then close your eyes and mentally review the details of the picture of what you want to materialize. Finally, watch yourself; whenever your mind wanders, bring your attention back to your mental image.

As explained previously, see this picture as a present reality. Give your full attention to bringing the details into your vision. If you are not "eye-minded," you may find yourself reciting a description of the details of your image instead of visualizing them. Try, however, to call up pictures that correspond to the words. The more you try, the more definite the images will become.

Begin with the more significant features of the mental image. Then, after you have sketched these main outlines, go on to the details. Although in the early stages of your practice, the five-minute concentration period may pass before you have completed the picture, be sure to stop at the end of five minutes.

The next day begins with a quick review of what you did the previous day. Then pick up where you left off and develop the picture as much as possible in five minutes. Continue, day by day, until you have completed your mental pattern of the desired result.

By beginning with a quick review of your work's main outlines and details, you will have time to cover any additional information before the end of the five minutes.

Time spent in review is not counted toward the five minutes. Yet, it need not take long. The five minutes are devoted to adding *something* to your previous work.

Like everything else we learn, the first steps in this practice are the slowest. However, if possible, by keeping at it regularly, early in the morning, you will soon gain proficiency before taking up the day's routine. Before long, you can summon the entire image in less than five minutes, from its main features to the smallest details.

As you continue this practice over the coming years, you can form new images more easily and more quickly. This is one of the most valuable skills you can acquire.

During your morning practice, keep thoughts of the future out of your consciousness. You are creating a mental pattern that already exists. No matter what your external circumstances may be, your mental image is part of those circumstances. If you watch what occurs while you make mental pictures, you will discover that you, who make the images and observe them, are at the center of your spiritual field, as you are at the center of the physical area surrounding your body. Therefore, your mental images are part of your environment, as are the physical objects outside your body.

More Laws of Subconsciousness

Your field of mental imagery is the controlling factor in your circumstances. Though you cannot trace connections between your mental images of the past and present conditions, *today's state is the result of the images from your yesteryears.*

Subconscious responses to mental imagery shape your present circumstances. Your future will be the materialization of what you imagine now.

By shifting your mental imagery from negative to positive, you set in motion forces that will make your world what you want it to be. Select *one objective*, visualize it, and follow these directions to transfer it to your subconscious. The result will be that your actual experiences will align with your mental patterns. Remember the law:

Thought takes form in action unless canceled by an opposing idea. Mental images tend to materialize.

The morning practice may be repeated whenever you have a few minutes to spare. As with most people, you will find it far better to use your mind creatively than merely to let it drift. Whenever negative states of mind assert themselves, you have mental patterns ready to counteract them. This will prove to be of great advantage.

Long ago, it was discovered that the way to overcome undesirable, doubting, pessimistic states of mind is to call their opposites into the field of consciousness. You don't have to shovel out darkness. Turn on the light. Trying to get rid of dark thoughts by force or suppressing them is a waste of time and effort. Instead, spend all your energy building positive states. They will automatically overcome the negatives. When you have built a mental pattern expressing heartfelt desire, you have the best protection against negative mental activities that waste energy and lead to failure.

Your morning practice makes it easier to call up positive imagery. You will soon reach a stage of development where it will be easy to think positive, constructive thoughts.

All this practice aims to perfect a *single clear image*. Single images are the only ones with sufficient power to penetrate deeply into the subconscious and to set in motion the hidden process that leads to materialization.

Relaxation Exercise Before Bed

This exercise is to be undertaken at night, after you have gone to bed, turned out the light, and made yourself thoroughly comfortable. This practice will enable you to transfer the image to the subconscious.

The first requirement for success is physical relaxation. To achieve this, begin at your toes. Tense them a little. This will focus your consciousness on the motor cells in your brain, which control your feet. As soon as you have done this, relax all the muscles in your feet.

Next, focus on the muscles of your legs between the knees and the ankles. Tense them a little, then relax. Follow this by tensing and relaxing the muscles between the knees and the hips.

Now take a deep breath, then tense your abdominal muscles while holding your breath. Then exhale and relax the abdominal muscles. Next, take another breath, this time tense, and relax the muscles across the chest. Relax as you exhale.

Now tense the muscles across the small of the back, and then relax them. Next, follow the same procedure with the muscles across your shoulders.

Next, relax your hands, forearms, and upper-arm muscles using the same procedure. After this, relax your neck muscles.

Then tense the facial muscles vigorously and relax them completely.

We provide these directions in detail to ensure you understand that tension must precede relaxation. Tension stimulates the activity of the cells in the motor centers, which control the muscles.

Relaxation is control, not of the muscles themselves, so much as of the nerve force which energizes them and of the brain centers which distribute this nerve force.

By all-over relaxation, you can contact the physical centers of the subconscious that link the conscious mind to the deeper subconscious centers. For example, the brain cells that control your muscles are unconscious, as are any other powers of that hidden mental field.

By relaxation, you can draw the nerve force at will away from any part of the voluntary muscular system. This practice gives you an extraordinary command of body and mind.

At the end of the relaxation exercise, you are ready to transfer your one image into your subconscious. Summon the image before your mind's eye, clearly. You may see it in the darkness, a foot or so in front of your eyes. Or you may be one of those who see their mental images between the eyes and the closed eyelids. With eyes closed, others see the picture in a mental space behind the forehead.

Visualization

Imagine that you are printing this picture on your brain's cells at the BACK OF YOUR HEAD1. This is easier than it may seem. After a few tries, you will get the knack of mentally carrying the picture to the back of your brain and fixing it there.

Here is an example: you never try to deceive the subconscious. The occipital lobe in the brain is the sight center. It is at the back of the head. The cells of the sight center are those whose activity provides you with all your visual images. When you seem to carry the image back into the brain, you are mentally following the course of the light rays, which imprint visual images on sight cells at the back of your head.

After you have completed the exercise, prepare for sleep. If the mental work has left you wakeful, go through your relaxation procedure again. Then dismiss further thoughts about your aim. If those ideas recur, turn your attention to a pleasant incident from your past and dwell on it. The main thing is to stop conscious thoughts about your aim before falling asleep.

Chapter 6 Notes

The Brain

The occipital lobe is the brain's visual processing center, containing most of the visual cortex. So we literally see with the backs of our heads.

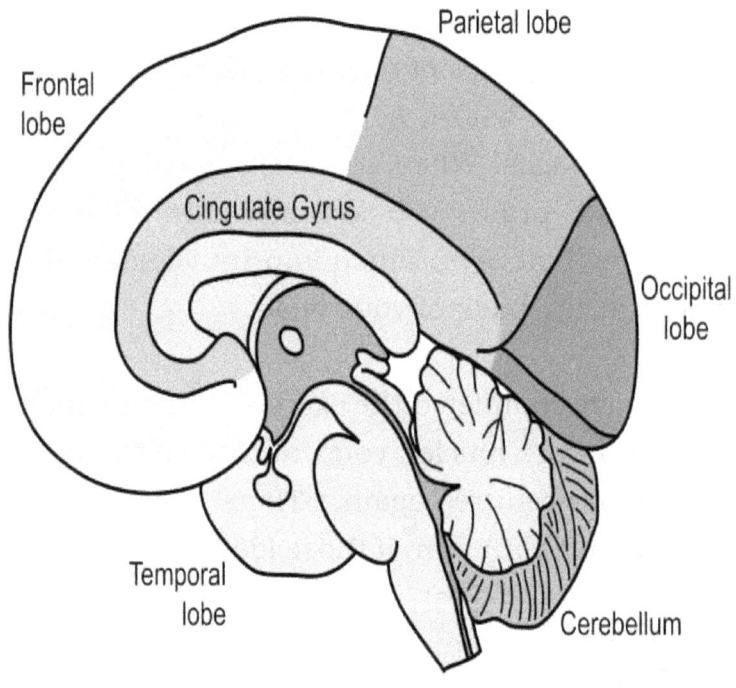

By NEUROtiker - Own work, CC BY-SA 3.0,
https://commons.wikimedia.org/w/index.php?curid=2653584

CHAPTER 7 – Review

Let's begin with a review of the powers of the subconscious.

1. *The subconscious is the bodybuilder. It cures every disease. This curative power may be aroused by mental methods, which often succeed when other means for stirring the subconscious have failed.*

2. *The subconscious stores our memories. It records all our experiences and summarizes the essentials of the race experience. This record of the race experience is the true source of most of our intuitions, and many scientific "discoveries" are recoveries from it.*

3. *Subconsciousness makes connections. It links us to who we need to be and who we want to be, to doing what we want to do and having what we want.*

4. *The subconscious operations are controllable from the conscious level, provided the correct methods are used.*

The powers of the subconscious and methods of control are not new. Some of the methods are very ancient.

For centuries, the details of this ancient technique for accessing the subconscious and releasing its forces were kept secret by small groups of initiates. Generation after generation, only a few were admitted to these exclusive circles of the wise. Methods for harnessing the powers of the subconscious were taught to these pupils under strict obligations of secrecy.

The transmission of this ancient knowledge has continued to this day. Since the great awakening to occult truths in the last quarter of the nineteenth century, much information that was once held in reserve is now public. The custodians of the Inner Wisdom now permit teachings to be communicated to all who seek. This course and others are open instructions derived from the secret tradition.

The Subconscious Responds Best to Visual Suggestions.

The technique for controlling the subconscious forces was formulated about seven hundred years ago by members of a branch of the Inner School who met in the intellectual center of the world—the city of Fez, in Morocco. From their meetings, it was discovered that,

Subconsciousness responds more to visual images than to any other form of suggestion.

Of all our senses, sight is the most highly developed. A Chinese proverb says, "One picture is worth ten thousand words." Suppose a Chinese, a Frenchman, and an American who understand only their native tongue look at the same tree. They all know what it is, and the subconscious associations of ideas evoked by the image will be nearly the same.

Every visual image has its fixed subconscious responses. For example, look at a picture of a tree and write down the ideas that arise in your mind. Continue this experiment for two or three days. Your list of associations will be similar in many respects to what any other person in the world would write.

Because every visual image elicits a subconscious response, pictures designed according to the laws of subconscious association may depend on evoking predictable responses. No matter who looks at them, the designs will always call up the same associations of ideas once their influence sinks below the personal level of reaction. Even when one does not know the inner meaning of such a picture or mistakes its real significance at first, the subconscious response will be called forth, provided one looks at the image often and attentively.

The Pictorial Tarot

Based on this fact, an ancient technique was developed. This method for accessing and releasing subconscious powers consists of repeated acts of attention to a series of visual images. The pictures automatically produce subconscious reactions.

It is better to know beforehand what each picture means. When we understand why a design elicits a definite subconscious reaction, the effect occurs more quickly because the conscious expectation adds to the visual image's suggestive power.

Looking at a set of pictures is the basis of this technique for evoking and directing the subconscious forces. The twenty-two pictures are known as the *Keys of Tarot*. (Tarot is pronounced approximately TEAR-oh, with the first syllable accented and rhyming with bear.) Each of these pictures is an ingenious combination of visual images that correspond psychologically. Hence, each Tarot Key calls forth a specific subconscious response. The reaction is partly mental and physiological because each picture sets in motion an unconscious deductive process that modifies hidden activities that condition all physical body states and functions.

The first Tarot Key (The Fool) is designed to awaken subconscious contact with superconscious power sources and vision. The second Key (The Magician) calls forth mental and physical states favorable to concentration and alerts one to one's environment.

The third picture (The High Priestess) brings into operation forces that find expression in memory and recollection. The fourth (The Empress) induces the mental and bodily conditions required for creative imagination. And so on, through the mental activities needed to produce a balanced, well-rounded personality.

Our wise predecessors discovered that all modes of human consciousness and personality powers fall into twenty-two principal classes. After extensive experiments, they determined that combinations of pictorial imagery will activate each of the twenty-two fundamental powers. They then submitted their findings to a group of artists among their members, who designed the twenty-two Tarot Keys.

Two versions were produced. One was crude and intentionally left incomplete. Nevertheless, they were accurate enough for initiates familiar with the elaborate version that was not in circulation. The esoteric Tarot Keys were shown at regular meetings to members of the School who invented the Tarot.

The crude version was disguised as a game. This enabled the initiated to use the Keys in public without being suspected of being students of knowledge proscribed by the ignorant bigots in power.

Secrecy was necessary for studying practical psychology because anything out of the ordinary was attributed to the devil. Nevertheless, the game won instant popularity, and the Tarot became the source of our pack of playing cards.

The secret version of the Tarot has been used by the Inner School since the 1200s. It was hinted at in *Fama Fraternitatis* and in the early Rosicrucian book. In *Fama*, the Tarot is described as ROTA, one of the fraternity's most valued possessions. TAROT is an artificial word that transposes the syllables of ROTA (Latin for wheel) and adds an extra "T" as a blind. These wonderful pictures have exercised a tremendous, if little-known, influence on humanity.

Eliphas Levi says,

The Tarot is a true oracle that answers all possible questions with precision and infallibility. A prisoner with no other book than the Tarot, if he knew how to use it, could, in a few years, acquire a universal science and speak on all subjects with unequaled learning and inexhaustible eloquence.

An eminent Russian philosopher, Ouspensky, author of *Tertium Organum*, says,

There are many methods for developing the 'sense of symbols' in those striving to understand the hidden forces of Nature and Humanity, and for teaching the fundamental principles and elements of the esoteric language. The most synthetic and interesting of these methods is the Tarot.

Tarot summarizes the Hermetic Sciences—the Kabala, Alchemy, Astrology, and Magic. These sciences form a single system for an extensive, in-depth psychological investigation of man's nature, encompassing the world of noumenon (God, the world of Spirit) and the world of phenomena (the visible, physical world). The letters of the Hebrew alphabet and the various allegories of the Kabala; the names of metals, acids, and salts in alchemy; and the names of good and evil spirits in magic—all these were intended only to veil the truth from the uninitiated.

Freemasonry is one of the few surviving remnants of the ancient psychological system, though few Masons know the treasure they have inherited from the past. General Albert Pike, Grand Commander of the Southern Jurisdiction of the Scottish Rite in the United States, says,

"He who desires to attain to an understanding of the Grand Word and the possession of the Great Secret must follow the order indicated in the alphabet of the Tarot to classify his acquisitions of knowledge and direct the operation."— Morals and Dogmas, p. 777.

What is the Grand Word? Its essential meaning is human. What is the Great Secret? It directs the hidden forces of human inner life, the potencies of the subconscious. The operation is called the Great Work. The Tarot Keys are a valuable means for enabling us to carry out this operation because each Tarot picture calls forth specific powers from the subconscious depths.

This week, test your grasp of the material by answering the questions at the end of this lesson.

The next course in our curriculum will be the beginning of your Tarot studies. By the time you finish it, you will have a complete set of Tarot Keys. Use them as directed in the lessons, and you will make real progress in harnessing the subconscious's powers. The next lesson series is Introduction to the Tarot, with the booklet Highlights of Tarot.

Chapter 7 Notes

Summary of Technique

What do you want?

Take time to sort through all the external demands and expectations placed on you and find what you really want.

This takes time; don't hurry, but don't procrastinate. Make haste slowly.

Once you know what you want, list what it looks like, tastes like, smells like, feels like, and sounds like. Then, see yourself in the activity. Finally, talk it out in the car or somewhere where you are alone.

Tell no one about your one aim. Instead, remember the magician's motto, TO KNOW, TO WILL, TO DARE, AND TO BE SILENT.

Imagination

See yourself performing an activity around what you want—daydream.

Create a symbol or a single image that represents your One Aim.

A symbol is a mental construct of your desire that is meaningful to you. It does not need to be a conventional symbol. It can be as simple as a number.

The symbol should be one that you can summon in your mind's eye quickly and with minimal effort.

Transferring the Image to the Subconsciousness

Upon waking and before bed (between waking and sleeping), summon the image and transfer it to the back of the head (the subconscious center of the brain).

Faith

Have a confident expectation that what you want will come. *Feel* your one aim in the present.

Find ways to strengthen your faith in your abilities. Then reward yourself when you succeed.

The Magical Vision

Do you have the eyes to see that what you want has come to you?

Things rarely work out exactly as you expect. Reality and expectations are seldom, if ever, the same. Learn to recognize your successes, even partial ones, and then acknowledge your achievement.

TEST

Please answer the following questions as briefly as possible while maintaining clarity.

1. Have you formulated your first objective?

2. Have you planned the steps needed to achieve it?

3. Do you understand which forms of bodily activity are required to realize your One Aim?

4. Can you form clear mental images?

5. How do you define the subconscious?

6. What danger arises from the peculiarity of the subconscious reasoning process?

7. What value does silence have?

8. What success have you had since starting this work?

PAUL FOSTER CASE BOOKS

1. SEVEN STEPS IN PRACTICAL OCCULTISM

2. AN INTRODUCTION TO THE TAROT AND ASTROLOGY

3. TAROT FUNDAMENTALS

4. TAROT INTERPRETATIONS

5. THE MASTER PATTERN

6. THE THIRTY-TWO PATHS OF WISDOM

7. THE TREE OF LIFE

8. THE NEOPHYTE RITUALS OF PAUL FOSTER CASE

9. THE ATTUNEMENT RITUALS OF PAUL FOSTER OF CASE

10. THE SECOND ORDER RITUALS OF PAUL FOSTER CASE

11. THE NEOPHYTE GRADE WORK OF PAUL FOSTER CASE.

12. THE ZELATOR GRADE WORK OF PAUL FOSTER CASE.

13. THE THEORICUS GRADE WORK OF PAUL FOSTER CASE.

14. THE PRACTICUS GRADE WORK OF PAUL FOSTER CASE.

WADE COLEMAN BOOKS

1. SEPHER SAPPHIRES Volume 1

2. SEPHER SAPPHIRES Volume 2

3. THE ASTROLOGY WORKBOOK

4. MAGIC OF THE PLANETS

5. THE MAGICAL PATH

6. THE ZODIAC OF DENDARA EGYPT

7. ATHANASIUS KIRCHER'S QUADRIVIUM

To contact the author,

DENDARA_ZODIAC@protonmail.com

BIBLIOGRAPHY

Anonymous, *Egyptian Texts of the Bronze Book*. Your Own World Books Inc., 2005.

Atwood, Mary Anne. *A Suggestive Inquiry into the Hermetic Mystery with a Dissertation on the More Celebrated of the Alchemical Philosophers, being an attempt towards the recovery of the Ancient Experiment of Nature.* With an Introduction by Walter Leslie Wilmshurst. Belfast: William Tait, 1918.

Pike, Albert. *Morals and Dogma of the Ancient and Accepted Scottish Rite.* Charleston, NC: L.H. Jenkins, 1947.

www.ingramcontent.com/pod-product-compliance
Lightning Source LLC
Chambersburg PA
CBHW060357050426
42449CB00009B/1784